Skills for OU St

Thinking Critically

The Open University Walton Hall, Milton Keynes MK7 6AA

The Open University is incorporated by Royal Charter (RC 000391), an exempt charity in England & Wales and a charity registered in Scotland (SC 038302).

Edited, designed and typeset by The Open University.

Printed in the United Kingdom by Thanet Press.

ISBN 978-0-7492-2920-7

1.1

Skills for OU Study

Thinking Critically

Critical thinking is an essential part of successful study at university. In this booklet you will discover what critical thinking is and how to do it. This booklet accompanies the *Skills for OU Study* website http://www.open.ac.uk/skillsforstudy, which contains advice, quizzes and exercises to help you.

Contents

1 Critical thinking and why it is important

Thinking critically as a student will confer benefits in many areas of your life. Critical thinking skills are a vital part of your academic life – when reading, when writing and when working with other students.

You probably already use critical thinking skills in domestic decision-making or at work – for example, when you are choosing car insurance or assessing how to move forward in a project. Now you need to transfer these skills to academic life. This booklet will show you how to do that effectively.

1.1 What is critical thinking?

To think critically is to examine ideas, evaluate them against what you already know and make decisions about their merit. The aim of critical thinking is to try to maintain an 'objective' position. When you think critically, you weigh up all sides of an argument and evaluate its strengths and weaknesses. So, critical thinking skills entail:

- actively seeking all sides of an argument
- testing the soundness of the claims made
- testing the soundness of the evidence used to support the claims.

Because your aim when thinking critically is to *respond objectively* to what you are reading or thinking through, you need to keep an open mind and be prepared to question the author's claims. How you do this and the questions you ask will vary depending on what – and why – you are reading (for example, you might be responding to an assignment question). As a result, you must always be prepared to adapt your approach according to the demands of the material.

As you read through your course materials you will pick up some of the terminology that Open University academics use to communicate the objectiveness of their reasoning. Pinpoint the words they use to indicate a balanced approach to the topic. For example, you will notice that phrases such as:

- 'it can be argued that'
- 'tends to' and
- 'there is evidence to suggest that'

… convey a certain amount of restraint. Look out for other examples of phrases you can use in your own writing.

1.2 Why is critical thinking so important?

The type of evidence varies between disciplines – in Arts subjects, it may be the close reading of a text; in Science it will more likely be a set of data.

For an author, writing academically means that she or he must be able to defend an argument against charges such as bias, lack of supporting evidence or incompleteness. Critical thinking enables you as a reader to assess the evidence in what you are reading and identify spurious or illogical reasoning.

Thinking critically will also help you to create strong arguments of your own (for example, in assignments). This means that you will be able to present and justify any claims you make based on the evidence you have evaluated.

If you learn and practise effective critical thinking skills early on in your studies with the OU, they will contribute at many levels in your academic life. When reading, they will allow you to understand the content of your course clearly. You will be able to analyse and evaluate – and compare and contrast – the value of particular materials, including theories, methods, concepts and the major debates that have been presented.

You may find thinking in a critical way quite difficult at first, but rest assured it gets easier the more you practise it.

Developing critical thinking skills will allow you to develop more reasoned arguments for your assignments, projects and examination questions. You will be able to use and draw on evidence to justify your own arguments and ideas. In addition, you will be able to synthesise your own thoughts, the thoughts of differing theorists/researchers and those of the course materials authors.

1.3 Being an independent learner

All universities encourage their students to be 'independent learners' and critical thinking is central to this. You show you are an independent learner when you analyse, evaluate and synthesise information from a variety of sources and present your own justified interpretation. This is known as employing 'higher order thinking skills'.

You may encounter some activities during your study that don't require high levels of critical thinking. For example, some multiple-choice questions might simply elicit your knowledge and understanding of your topic. However, essay- and report-style assignments frequently demand interpretation and synthesis skills. Part of this is using 'higher order thinking skills'. These are the skills used to analyse and manipulate information (rather than just memorise it). In the 1950s, Benjamin Bloom identified a set of important study and thinking skills for university students, which he called the 'thinking triangle' (Bloom, 1956: see Figure 1).

Much of university education and assessment has been greatly influenced by these ideas.

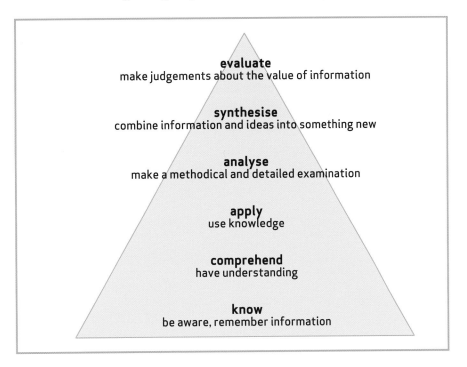

Figure 1   Levels of intellectual skill: the thinking triangle.
Source: adapted from Bloom, 1956

These higher-order thinking skills are the same as critical thinking skills. They will help you in both your reading and writing, and enable you to work effectively as an independent learner. They will also, as you will see in Section 4, help you to work with others in a constructive and useful way.

2 Reading with a critical eye

As with any new skills you develop, it may take some time to become comfortable with thinking critically about what you read and write. However, the more you practise it the better you will become. In this section you will learn how to read using critical thinking skills.

2.1 Using enquiry-based learning

Critical thinking requires concentration, so try to find a quiet place to study and do it in 'bite-sized' chunks, giving yourself breaks between.

As an independent learner you must be willing to reflect on what you are doing and how you are progressing. Asking appropriate questions of the materials you are reading is an essential part of this. You won't exercise your critical thinking skills by listening or reading passively. You will gain these skills only by engaging actively with the subject matter. You can do this by asking appropriate questions of the material, investigating solutions to any problems, creating new understanding as a result and then reflecting on what you have gained. This is called enquiry-based learning.

Taking a reflective, enquiry-based approach to your study helps you delve deeper into the materials you read (see Figure 2). It requires you to keep an open mind, ask questions and reflect upon the answers you might come up with.

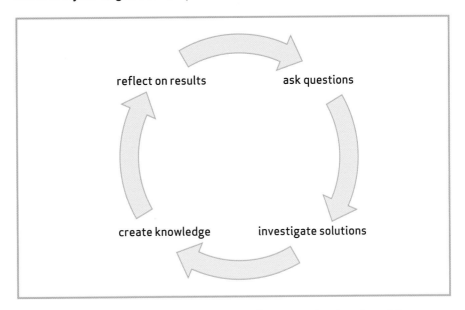

Figure 2   The enquiry cycle encourages deeper understanding of the subjects you read about

In some study disciplines, critical thinking is used particularly in the formal evaluation or construction of an 'argument'. Knowing what constitutes an argument will help you identify what is happening when someone makes an inadequate argument.

2.2 What is an 'argument'?

An argument can be said to have four basic elements: (i) a claim, (ii) evidence, (iii) a warrant and (iv) any qualifications to the argument that might be necessary (see Figure 3). The nature of the argument made determines the exact form in which these elements appear.

This is based on the Toulmin system of argumentation, developed during the 1950s (Toulmin, 1958), which has since been updated and adapted (Booth et al., 1995).

The claim: this is the point that is being made; what is being argued for. When you read your course materials, ask yourself if it is relevant to your current needs (i.e. can you use it in your assignment, is it an important addition to your general knowledge of the subject?).

The evidence: this is the grounds upon which the claim is made. Sometimes it might be data from a study, other times it might be a quote or reference to someone else's published work. You will hear it referred to as the 'supporting evidence'. The evidence needs to fully support the claim being made or, if it doesn't, its weaknesses need to be acknowledged and dealt with in some way (for example, by 'qualifications').

The warrant: this is the general principle that forms the bridge between the claim and the evidence it is based on. It is logical reasoning that connects the evidence to the claim.

Qualifications: these are concessions that may have to be made within an argument that limit what someone might be able to claim (see 'evidence' above).

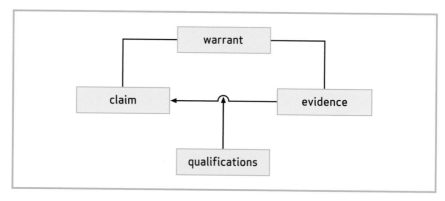

Figure 3   The elements of an argument and how they relate to each other

Seeing what a badly constructed argument looks like can help you think about how you would have done it better. Examine the argument in the following box and think about why you might find it unconvincing:

An example of a flawed argument

Claim: I won't have to work so hard if I go to my first tutorial.

Evidence: OU statistics show that students who attend the first tutorial are more likely to pass the course.

Warrant: The statistics say that attending the first tutorial makes you likely to pass the course. I will attend the tutorial and feel confident that that will secure me success.

Qualifications: I need to ensure that the tutor notices that I've attended.

The example given above is a flawed argument. There *are* statistics that suggest students who attend the first tutorial are more likely to pass the course and this feels factual. However, be careful of attaching a cause and effect relationship to this. For example, attending tutorials = success.

The qualification reveals that the writer believes that mere attendance secures success. This makes the argument imbalanced because it hasn't explored adequately other reasons why the association between success and attending the first tutorial exists. Is it likely that, given the aim of university education to produce students who can discuss a subject authoritatively with their peers, merely showing up at a classroom will ensure those students a pass? No … it is more likely that attendance will allow them an opportunity to listen to and think about useful discussions and explanations. Attendance in itself doesn't guarantee good marks. So the warrant doesn't link the evidence logically to the claim being made.

In order to think about this argument *critically*, you would ask the following questions:

- What else contributes to success?

- What are the characteristics of students who attend tutorials? For example, do they have more time to study and is this the factor that gives them the edge?

- What is it about tutorials that may make a difference? Could this be achieved another way?

2.3 A process for thinking critically

The aim of critical thinking is to try to maintain an 'objective' position. This means that you should try to be aware of any preconceptions you have that might be skewing the way you think about an argument. As you read, allow yourself opportunities to check your understanding and revisit sections if you are unsure of their meaning.

Although there is no one 'right' way of thinking critically, you will find it useful to get some basic tasks done before moving on to an evaluation of any material. Try the following three steps:

1   Identify the thrust of the information.

2   Analyse the material.

3   Compare and apply the information.

Identify the thrust of the information

First, identify the general thrust of the argument within the information you are reading. At this stage you are simply trying to define and be aware of the subject matter. Try to identify the:

* main points of the argument

* claims being made

* evidence used

* conclusions reached.

Analyse the material

As you read, think about whether or not the material is relevant to your needs. Here are some questions that might help in your analysis:

* Does the information make sense in relation to other theories and research? Where in the broader picture does this particular argument sit?

* How old is the material?

* Is the material clear or do you need to find additional information to aid your understanding?

* Can you identify any implications that might require you to look for other material? (Perhaps complementary explanations of a phenomenon if the original material is not comprehensive enough.)

- Does the argument present a balanced view or is the author disregarding some topics in order to put forward a particular argument?

Compare and apply information

Assignment questions will often ask you to apply theories, principles or formulae to situations. The process of trying to apply what you are learning can help you to build your understanding of the subject. Try looking for:

- the implications of one piece of information for another

- weaknesses that might be revealed when you apply the idea to a real-life situation

- a lack of coverage. Does the theory or formula only go so far and do you need to draw upon another theory or principle to complete your understanding of something?

2.4 How to evaluate an argument

When you evaluate academic material such as a journal article, you are aiming to form a judgement on the validity of the argument presented. You can do this by looking at the:

- coherence of the argument and

- the supporting evidence.

Coherence

Being able to identify when an argument is valid (i.e. that the claims made support the conclusions drawn adequately and justifiably) is vital.

- Check the line of reasoning – is it coherent and logical? Are there any flaws in its progression?

- Look at the conclusions drawn – are they supported adequately by the claims made throughout the argument? Are they 'valid' and do they make sense?

- Have the authors justified their claims by supporting them with acceptable sources of evidence?

- Are any assumptions made and, if so, are they acceptable?

- Have all alternative claims been considered? Is there any bias in the claims and supporting arguments?

- Is there any indication that a claim made is merely the author's opinion rather than based on evidence?

- Does the claim make sense when compared to the evidence used?

Supporting evidence

You also need to evaluate the evidence you have been presented with to establish its worth, in its own right and when compared with other evidence (see Figure 4).

- Does the evidence support all of the claims made? (Is it comprehensive?)

- Is the evidence appropriate for the topic?

- Is the evidence recent and is that important for your purposes?

- How does this evidence compare with that provided by other people: does it conflict with other evidence? Is it complementary to other evidence? Does it co-exist, adding something extra to the topic?

- Are there any methodological issues about the collection of the evidence that might impinge upon its usefulness?

Figure 4 The quality of evidence relates directly to the nature of the data and how it is interpreted

2.5 Taking notes critically

Being able to express your powers of critical thinking begins with the notes that you take during your course. Note taking is an important stage in understanding what you are reading. You may find that the very act of writing your notes helps you to distil your understanding.

The questions you ask yourself as you take notes vary according to the nature of the materials and what you are trying to achieve. What you should try to achieve is a logical, objective interpretation of the argument you are presented with. When it comes to presenting arguments in your assignments, you need to be able to defend your point of view against charges such as bias, lack of supporting evidence, incompleteness and illogical reasoning. Using critical thinking when you take notes from course materials in the first place and then rigorously employing it when you construct your own line of argument in your assignments will help you avoid these problems.

Figure 5 demonstrates how you might structure your note taking. Use this example as inspiration to create your own template. You may, for example, want to add a category such as 'useful quotes'.

Remember, the questions you bear in mind as you read will change according to the nature of the subject matter or what you are trying to achieve. So take the categories used in Figure 5 as examples that you can change to suit your purposes.

| Topic: |
| Source: (e.g. author, book title, page number, edition) |
| Description |
| Claims |
| Evidence for claims |

Strengths	Weaknesses

| Questions and queries |
| Links to other topics |

Figure 5   Introducing critical thinking into your note taking

3 Writing with a critical voice

Not only do you have to *read* with a critical eye but you must also be able to express your ideas in a critical way. This means that your writing must demonstrate your understanding of the significance of an argument or perspective, the relevance of evidence and the strength of conclusions made.

3.1 How to approach to the question

Make sure you look at your tutor's feedback on your last assignment. Acting on this is central to being a self-reflective and independent learner.

Unless told otherwise, you are generally expected to draw upon your course materials for evidence when answering assignments and exam questions. As with your reading, you should try to engage actively with the assignment question and its required content. Again, you must apply a critical-thinking approach.

You can approach the question by:

* checking the notes that accompany the question in the assignment booklet

* splitting the question into bite-sized chunks

* looking closely at the 'process words' in the assignment title

* allowing some time to plan before you start writing and then some time to review what you've written afterwards

* making sure that you keep to the question set by referring back to it as you write.

3.2 Reading the question critically

When reading the assignment question, you can use your critical thinking skills to make sure that you understand the question fully. For instance, if the question asks you to 'compare and contrast' two different approaches, you will know that you have to devote some of your word count to one approach and some to the other. Likewise, if the question asks you to 'Assess the value of … to our understanding of…' you will have two points of focus in your answer.

Look to the **process words**. They will tell you what you are expected to do with the subject and are often verbs (such as 'compare and contrast'). You will find that the process words in your assignment questions prompt certain areas of critical thinking. So, for example, if the question asks you to:

- **Evaluate, assess, defend, support**: you will need to prepare a reasoned judgement based on your analysis.

- **Apply, demonstrate, illustrate, interpret, solve**: you will need to apply the subject (to a given situation).

- **Develop, formulate, arrange**: you are expected to combine the material with other materials you read in the course.

- **Compare, contrast, discriminate, distinguish, examine**: you will need to analyse the argument.

- **Define, list, name, order**: you will need to identify the content.

These verbs may have meanings that are quite specific within your subject area! *Always* consult your assignment booklet carefully to make sure you know what is expected of you. If you are still in doubt, ask your tutor.

The box below and the following text demonstrate an example of how you might approach a level 3 computing course assignment question.

Using critical thinking in an assignment

(a) Write about 300 words outlining the differences between robots built according to the SENSE–ACT model and those built according to the older SENSE–PLAN–ACT model. Describe the relative strengths and weaknesses of each model.

(b) In Unit 4, we categorised learning strategies under four broad headings: supervised, reinforcement, imitation and evolution. Use the Web to find an original example of one of these used in an actual system. Write a set of notes, describing in outline the example you found, and sketching the main features of the learning process as it was implemented. Aim to write no more than 200 words.

A good place to start would be to split part (a) of this question into two chunks. There are two process words used in the question that help with this: 'outline' and 'describe'. For the first chunk, you only need to talk about differences between the two models rather than describe the whole model in each case. You might, however, write a description of each model first to help you identify where they differ.

For the second chunk, some critical thinking is required. You need to compare the two models again but this time you must form an opinion about which aspects of each model are advantages and which aspects are drawbacks. It's possible that some aspects may be a strength in some circumstances and a weakness in others, in which case you may need to give examples to illustrate these ideas.

For part (b) you might be tempted to plunge straight into searching the web for a useful example. A far better approach would be to spend a bit of time thinking about the four learning strategies and making some notes on them to be absolutely sure you understand what concepts to look for in an actual system. The key process word for this part is once again 'describe'. It may be tricky to find an example that can be outlined, and its learning strategy described, in only 200 words. You would need to carefully evaluate the results of your web search to decide which system offers the best opportunity to demonstrate your understanding of the concepts.

The above discussion has hopefully shown you that it is worth spending some time thinking about, planning and researching your answers to assignment questions.

3.3 Using structuring devices in your writing

In addition to structuring your assignment as an essay-style or a report-style assignment, you must convey the overall logic and progression of your argument. This will demonstrate the critical thinking that underlies your assignment. As you gain experience you will find your own favourite writing patterns. In the meantime, here are some suggested ways of structuring your writing:

* use context and examples

* use themes

* link and signpost

Use context and examples

Your writing needs to involve a certain amount of contextualisation, which means that you define the background of the subject for your reader. You are likely to do this, in a general way, within your introduction but you may also need to set the context at various points throughout your assignment.

How you set the context will depend on your assignment. It may involve giving descriptions of theories and concepts, a historical account of attitudes or a description of a problem. Another way is to move between descriptions of particular phenomena to a more general and overarching perspective of your topic. This will help your reader recognise how your point is positioned within the subject as a whole. You might also change the focus as your argument unfolds. This can be a useful way of introducing perspective and contextualising your argument.

The quote in the box below is from a late chapter of Book 1 of the Social Sciences course, DD100. Here, the authors use a real-life example to explore the connection between people's private health and more public aspects of life.

From the general to the particular

The following is an extract from Smith and Goldblatt's chapter 'Whose health is it anyway?' in Hinchliffe and Woodward's book, *The Natural and the Social: Uncertainty, Risk, Change*.

> In Chapter 1 of this book Wendy Hollway discussed the way in which our natural biological make-up interacts with the kind of social circumstances in which we live in different areas of human experience and at different times. … as an asthma sufferer, I am only too aware of how my biology interacts with my social and physical environment … despite taking care, I sometimes get a full-blown attack and this affects my ability to take part in my normal everyday activities. … Controlling my asthma requires constant medication, so my 'illness' has a cost on the health service. Therefore, dealing with my asthma … is of interest not just to me, but also to the government and indeed to everyone who pays for and utilizes the health service. So, looking at the causes of health and illness and possible interventions offers another way in which we can explore how the natural interacts with the social conditions in which we live.

Source: Smith and Goldblatt, 2004, p.42

This sharp focus on an individual experience helps them to contextualise their argument that our biological make-up interacts with social circumstance. So you can see that moving from a broad argument to a particular example or piece of evidence helps them support their overarching argument.

There are other contextualising devices you might call upon to add structure to your writing. For example:

- Spatial organisation – for example a description of the molecular composition of a chemical.

- Temporal organisation – for example, the process of change over time that occurs within an ecological habitat (succession), or changes of attitudes towards something over time.

- From less complex to more complex – for example, from the make-up of a family unit to the make-up of the society in which they live.

Use themes

Examples of course themes are: 'uncertainty and diversity' in society (social sciences, level one) and 'chains and cycles' (science, openings course).

You may find that your course materials highlight certain 'themes' that run throughout the course. Your assignment question (or the notes that accompany it) may reference these themes explicitly or implicity.

Draw on themes to add structure to your writing. They can prove a useful device that might help you link different aspects of your course learning. Use them to demonstrate differences and similarities between schools of thought or theoretical approaches. You can also use a theme to help you to frame an argument or conclusion.

Link and signpost

Use linking words and signposting to connect your ideas. These make clear to your reader both how your argument progresses logically from one point to the next and how each new point is relevant. Here are some examples:

- Draw attention to certain points: 'equally importantly'; 'furthermore'.

- Indicate cause and effect progression: 'this results in'; 'consequently'; 'for this reason'.

- Indicate progression within an argument: 'therefore'; 'however' 'nevertheless'.

 Visit www.open.ac.uk/skillsforstudy for more on linking words.

3.4 Getting your critical thinking into your writing

Look back to Section 2.2 to remind yourself of the reasoning you need to use in arguments.

Where you are asked to propose an argument and draw conclusions in an assignment, you need to make a clear argument, identify your claims, present the relevant evidence and draw justified conclusions. You do this by showing clearly the theory or approach and evidence you are using to support your claims. Indicate how you have analysed and evaluated the theories in order to come to your conclusions. You will also need to make clear the steps in your thought processes and show how the different parts of your argument fit together to make a cohesive whole. Finally, you will show that your argument is balanced rather than just taking a stance from one point of view.

If you have been asked to comment on an argument and you think it is flawed then you must make a reasoned case and present evidence to support your views. If you introduce new ideas, draw them logically from the original material.

3.5 A process for getting critical thinking into your writing

* Examine how and where critical thinking might support your answer and any arguments you present.

* If you have drawn conclusions or identified implications, consider whether these should be included.

* Remember to link your ideas to evidence and ensure the 'warrant' is justifiable.

* If you draw inferences from someone else's argument, you will need to provide logical reasoning to back up your extrapolation.

* Once you have a first draft of your assignment then ask yourself whether there is enough evidence to support your claims. Do you need to rethink or tone down your argument with more objective language? Do you need to refute or rebut any objections to your argument?

* Less is more. Use your critical thinking skills to select the most appropriate content rather than putting in everything you have read on the topic.

This is all work you do as an independent learner. The next section outlines how you can use critical thinking when working with others.

4 Critical thinking and working with others

The skill of thinking critically sitting at your study desk with time to compose an argument is one thing, but the ability to argue effectively but objectively and professionally with another person will take your skills to a new level.

4.1 At tutorials

Sharing your ideas with other students in tutorials (and day or residential schools) provides you with an opportunity to practise your critical thinking skills. You can debate the alternative explanations and claims that other students have and defend your own standpoint.

You might feel nervous about joining in and putting forward your point of view. This is understandable, but developing an appreciation of what it takes to think critically about something can help a lot here.

The box below is based on an exercise from an OU course, AA308, Thought and Experience: Themes in the Philosophy of Mind. The discussion that follows the box unpacks some of the possible experiences you might have when you get involved in group work during tutorials.

Using critical thinking in a tutorial

Imagine that your tutor presents your group with the following set of words and asks you to consider the question 'What is an emotion?' Spend a few moments considering how you think this question could be answered.

nausea	hunger	love
disgust	fear	jealousy
cowardice	being startled	joy
feeling cheerful	nostalgia	sadness

It is likely that the group of students above would immediately agree on several words as representing an emotion, for example 'joy'. Even so, they can still debate their reasons for their choices, using this as an opportunity to practise putting forward their ideas, as well as listening to and weighing up the ideas of others.

More often than not at a tutorial you will not agree with the views of everyone else. Some students may declare that 'nausea' is an emotion; you may disagree. If you explain why you disagree and give examples to back up your case, then others can state where they differ. They may challenge your original thoughts, forcing you to re-evaluate your own claim. On reflection, you may stick to your original belief but re-evaluation has helped you to state your case more convincingly … or you may change your mind.

After the tutorial it is likely that some of the discussion points will stick in your mind. These could be those that you agreed with or, just as likely, those you disagreed with. So engaging in debate with your fellow students provides you with an opportunity to practise and strengthen your critical thinking skills. It also helps you to think through particular issues that might come up during assignments and examinations.

4.2 Using critical thinking in your course forum

Your critical thinking skills could be enhanced further by joining in with, or starting off, a discussion thread on your course forum. Not only would this allow you to formulate your ideas and justifications by writing them down but it would also expose your stance to a whole new set of students. It is likely that this new test of your ideas would throw up differing viewpoints to those at the tutorial and the circle of evaluation and re-evaluation can begin again.

4.3 Critical thinking and etiquette

Finally, bear in mind the usual rules of etiquette used in online forums and face-to-face tutorials. These are important to ensure that you manage to present your view in a positive and friendly way.

- Acknowledge another person's view before going on to challenge it.
- Be constructive in your challenge, rather than simply dismissing another's point of view.
- Reflect on what you consider to be the strengths of another person's argument.
- Think about your language and whether you run the risk of being inadvertently offensive before you speak.

5 Summary: thinking for yourself

Critical thinking skills are an intrinsic element in your study – in your reading, in writing your assignments and in working with others. Look through your course materials for specific guidance on how to apply critical thinking in your discipline, and remember that the sooner you start to develop these skills the greater the benefit they will bring.

Remember, critical thinking skills involve:

- actively seeking all sides of an argument
- testing the soundness of the claims made
- testing the soundness of the evidence used to support the claims.

You will take these skills with you throughout your student life and beyond into postgraduate study and your personal life. Being able to think critically about complex issues is enjoyable and an exciting skill to have.

As you practise and improve your abilities and your thinking becomes more acute and discerning you will experience the pleasure of becoming a truly independent learner and thinker.

Appendix

Glossary

Argument: the identification of one or more claims supported by logical reasoning and evidence which lead to a justified conclusion.

Claim: an idea or contention asserted in an argument.

Conclusion: the final position taken on a topic, based on the results of a critical evaluation and reflection about the claims and evidence presented.

Critical thinking: thinking based on logical reasoning and questioning, which enables you to reflect on the strengths and weaknesses of any evidence provided, draw logical conclusions and contribute new ideas to a topic.

Evaluation: an assessment of the validity of an argument.

Evidence: data, facts, information, studies etc. used to support claims, arguments and conclusions.

Implications: issues arising from a topic of study.

Inferences: ideas deduced from evaluating an argument.

Innovative: new and different ways in which a topic can be viewed and investigated.

Interpretation: an explanation of the meaning of something.

Justified interpretation: one that provides a balanced argument and refers to reliable evidence for the points made.

Qualification: concessions that may have to be made within an argument that limit what someone might be able to claim.

Reasoning: the process of forming conclusions and inferences.

Stance: your position on a topic based on the evidence you have evaluated.

Synthesise: draw together different strands of information making logical connections between them.

Warrant: logical reasoning that connects the evidence to the claim.

References

Bloom, B.S. (ed.) (1956) *Taxonomy of Educational Objectives. Handbook 1, Cognitive Domain*, London, Longman.

Booth, W., Colomb, G.G., Williams, J.M. (1995) 'Making good arguments: an overview', in *The Craft of Research*, The University of Chicago Press, London.

Furedi, F. (1998) *Culture of Fear: Risk-taking and the Morality of Low Expectation*, London, Cassell.

NSPCC (2006) *Child Homicides, Key Child Protection Statistics*, http://www.nspcc.org.uk/Inform/resourcesforprofessionals/Statistics/KeyCPStats/4_wda48747.html (accessed April 2008).

Smith, B. and Goldblatt, D. (2004) 'Whose health is it anyway?', in Hinchliffe, S. and Woodward, K., *The Natural and the Social: Uncertainty, Risk, Change* (2nd edn) Routledge/The Open University, Milton Keynes.

The Open University (2007) *AA308, Identifying Emotions*, http://openlearn.open.ac.uk/mod/resource/view.php?id=229270 (accessed April 2008).

Toulmin, S. (1958) *The Uses of Argument*, Cambridge University Press, Cambridge.

Further reading

Toulmin, S.E., Rieke, R.D. and Janik, A. (1984) *An Introduction to Reasoning* (2nd edn) New York, Macmillan Publishing.